PRAISE FOR
CROSSBONES ON MY LIFE

What is etched here in these poems is the testimony of a very vocal and aware witness. Upon reading this work, the inclination would be to crown Mason the rogue poet Laureate of San Francisco—but knowing Mason (which I have since they started sneaking into Gravy Train!!!! shows as a teen), I'm pretty sure they would promptly reject any such honor. This chapbook is not a sentimental vehicle for nostalgia, but chronicles (and dare I say it, mostly in earnest) the unique position or watching a small lifetime of social, political, economic, and, perhaps most importantly, internal changes from the vantage point of a stationary position.

I trust these poems' shape and voice because they read prophetically without being preachy, assured without being a complete dogmatic asshole about it, elevated, though not unfamiliar with the gutter, and above all: right and exact.

BRONTEZ PURNELL
author of *100 Boyfriends* and *Since I Laid My Burden Down*

Crossbones on My Life

Mason J.

NOMADIC PRESS

OAKLAND

111 FAIRMOUNT AVENUE
OAKLAND, CA 94611

BROOKLYN

475 KENT AVENUE #302
BROOKLYN, NY 11249

WWW.NOMADICPRESS.ORG

MASTHEAD

FOUNDING AND MANAGING EDITOR
J. K. FOWLER

ASSOCIATE EDITOR
MICHAELA MULLIN

EDITOR
NATASHA DENNERSTEIN

MISSION STATEMENT

Nomadic Press is a 501 (C)(3) not-for-profit organization that supports the works of emerging and established writers and artists. Through publications (including translations) and performances, Nomadic Press aims to build community among artists and across disciplines.

SUBMISSIONS

Nomadic Press wholeheartedly accepts unsolicited book manuscripts. To submit your work, please visit www.nomadicpress.org/submissions

DISTRIBUTION

Orders by trade bookstores and wholesalers:
Small Press Distribution,
1341 Seventh Street
Berkeley, CA 94701
spd@spdbooks.org
(510) 524-1668 / (800) 869-7553

Crossbones on My Life

This book was made possible by a loving community of chosen family and friends, old and new.

For author questions or to book a reading at your bookstore, university/school, or alternative establishment, please send an email to info@nomadicpress.org.

Cover artwork and author portrait by Arthur Johnstone

Published by Nomadic Press, 111 Fairmount Avenue, Oakland, CA 94611

First printing, 2021

LIBRARY OF CONGRESS CATALOGING-IN-PUBLICATION DATA

Mason J. 1988 –
Title: *Crossbones on My Life*
P. CM.
Summary: *Crossbones on My Life* borrows its title from an invocation by Assotto Saint and honors the memory of snap queens, black lesbians, gay latinos, two-spirit natives, feral city youth, trans icons, and 'round the way girls. This debut chapbook from Mason J. chronicles their first-hand experiences with the HIV pandemic, brown girlhood, and sexuality, urban development/gay meccas, queercore cruising, leather daddies, Ghostship, gender identity, hood life, love, loss of a hometown, and more.

[1. POETRY. 2. LGBTQIA+. 3. BLACK. 4. LOVE AND RELATIONSHIPS. 5. AMERICAN GENERAL] I. III. TITLE.

LIBRARY OF CONGRESS CONTROL NUMBER: 2021932310

ISBN: 978-1-7363963-1-5

Crossbones on My Life

Mason J.

NOMADIC PRESS

CONTENTS

PART 3: TECHIE BECKY AND START-UP STEVE

UNDERTOWS OF GRIEF
(POST-GHOST SHIP FREEWRITES) 2016

PART 4: GENDER SECESSIONISM

PART 5: FLOWERS FOR SNAP QUEENS

INTRODUCTION

First and foremost, this work would not exist without the things that made me: the SFUSD special education classes of the '90s, misogynoir, Foster Care, the Crack and HIV epidemics, sex worker angels, drag queens, generation hyphy, my chosen and adopted family, the people who acted as my lovers and friends in bars and bookstores across the nation, the internet relationships I've held for decades as a child raised by social networking and public libraries, the Vigil matriarchy and my Still Here SF family for without whom I would've never returned to writing. Frankly— many of these poems come from the support of SF sidewalks, queer open mics, Nomadic Press, and RADAR Productions, who always made space for me.

Although I wish I could take credit for all of these words, many are channeled ancestrally or via my detailed thoughts; others come from the minds of old Black folks I chat with on MUNI, Asians, and Pacific Islanders who raised me. Summer-workin' English soccer hooligans I've shot Jameson with in pubs during 7 am Premier League matches. Sitting on the steps of City Hall as the Frisco 5[00] chanted "Fire Chief Suhr!" while the Mayor hid; these words are lines found on cocktail napkins after nights of running through the streets with queers, baydestrians, mi gente, they are spray paint-stained pants, broken-hearted texts I never sent to people who considered me too sick, sad, crazy, or radical to love.

While it would have been most comfortable to climb into an ivory tower and fling myself toward an MFA in hopes of impressing enough of the right people and working the lecture circuit to be "queer famous," I've never been one for the suggested path. By choice, finance, ability, I've been both insulated and caught ass-out peeing in alleys after last-call; like many locals, my work belongs to the people and the cities all over the country that raise those like me.

One of the firsts poems I ever dictated at age four or five was about a gold-stealing leprechaun being hogtied and defenestrated to punish him for his love of money. Frankly, I think this fact says all you need to know about me and my work: suspense, fairy tale, anti-capitalism, morality, and a little S&M.

PART ONE:
SAN FRANCISCO

WESTERN ADDITION BLUES, 2015

North Bay.
Our Lady of Sorrows with sky grey eyes, pan dulce breasts, and mossy green thighs
so devastatingly beautiful that at her golden gate speckled feet
strangers from around the world come West to rest and reset (or leap to their deaths)
no companion for the faint-hearted and innocent
she stays hustlin' hard for the citizens
raised her kin tough, smart, and yet still tender
thirsty for seduction and sweet surrender
real sucka free love
from an iron fist in a velvet glove

South Bay.
like moths, they came seeking our city lights
feasted on our homes and hearts like parasites
the affluenza got most of us,
and those it didn't take, now quake with untreatable aches
a physical expression for the same oppression
an attempt to make anyone
who's been healthy and happy here foolishly welcome
the smallpox blankets and poisoned water they keep offering as concessions

East Bay.
once the sun sets behind her ear
syringes, police interference, fish in the bowl, and underpaid immigrants do her bidding
in the light, profiteering pirates stage crushing invasions
the second maybe third colonization
for a new generation

but you can always find her
sailing down the block
slanging coke white savior dreams
trying to end the property damage and cultural genocide
against a litany of saints and sinners
keeping guard over ghetto two-spirit sissies like me
all the old queens and firm-handed OGs who survived the chaos of the
50s, 60s, 70s, 80s, and 90s

HELICOPTERS IN 'HOODS, 2016

circling carrion corpses in Californian food deserts
flying low and slow in San Pancho's Excelsior, Mission, Bayview,
Lakeview, Vis Valley, HP, Double Rock, and Fillmore districts
hopping fare gates and ghost-riding across bridges to Marin City, Murder
Dubs, Fruitvale, Deep E, Haystack, Antioch, Rich, Fairfield, Vallejo, &
Sac

Oh! ghetto vulture, I know your predatory flight all too well
from my early birdbrained memories of eating dinner on the floor in
silence
doing homework in a bathtub while you zig-zag overhead
as I tried my best to avoid the snap, crackle, popping off shots going off
up the street
a migratory drive-by flight my fright took subconsciously
desensitized but traumatized destinations I was born knowing how to
arrive at
before flying the coop and being another black or brown birds, shot for
sport

filthy urban fowl, trilling short-circuited tin can chirps
shrieking cockatiel songs from the sky
as you recklessly shit shells onto cars

this a swan song for my first exposure
c-PTSD aka the ghetto bird flu
a twittering to say
I am sick of you sick of you
nevermore knowing whether to play dead
or be a dead bird at the bottom of a metal cage

SAN FRANCISCO AS GRANDMOTHER, 2020

San Francisco as Grandmother
if you are lucky enough to find the doorbell,
she'll let you stay with her for weeks
    [your whole life if you like]
you'll play Jacks, Hopscotch, Heats, One Foot Off the Gutter
Get scolded for forgetting to take the meat out of the freezer

This is your home
With WIIC cheese *quesadillas y frijoles* for breakfast
Kings Hawaiian Roll, Miracle Whip, and Turkey sandwiches before
dinner
Werther's Originals dropped into A&W root beer floats at bedtime

You don't have to love living with her if you don't want to
but you will rub grandmother's feet with peppermint lotion
pretend to enjoy violet candies
find ways to memorize every Jeopardy Daily Double and drama on Y&R
because she offers prayers in the face of danger
keeps vigil over her children long after the star-spangled banner plays
and will always have space for you, even if you have to move away
matriarchy is the heart of San Francisco
and although some will say she's dead
I know her heart hasn't stopped; she's just having seismic tremors

THE FRUIT MAN AT MIDTOWN, 2015

Betwixt a bowl of Kix with half a teaspoon of sugar and 90s cartoons, I run down several flights of stairs from my 3rd-floor apartment. To the fruit man. Silently rolling tree sap between my fingers from a nearby pine, I wait my turn while his ashy palms sift through strawberries, cherries, blueberries, nectarines. When he turns his back to calculate their prices, I discreetly nip at the untagged fruit until I'm caught berry-handed with a laugh, then chased away by fast ladies in satin pajamas and hair curlers. You know, those passionate neighborhood ladies so full of pheromones and ego they need double names like EllieMae, JessieLee, or BarbaraAnn. Although the fruit man is long gone, I can still taste the sweet and sour flavors of peachy skin, pear-shaped hips, and passionfruit lips. How I remember each of those ladies from which the fruit man could always take his pick.

DID YOU KNOW CALIFORNIA WAS NAMED AFTER A BLACK DYKE? 2014

If San Francisco could jump or swim from the second coming of
colonizers
I bet she wouldn't.
brazen as Queen Calafia riding atop a trained griffin to kill Christian
invaders
SF would not move to LA, the Pacific Northwest, Chicago, New
Orleans, NY; she would remain unbothered

Could you even fathom her radiant but elusive radicles?
Raised potted and displaced.
bonsai
cacti
aloe plants
poppies
irises
black magic petunias
dancing-lady orchids
once rooted now cut and repotted
flora and fauna trampled under the feet of *guerlitos*
flower children loyal to their soil
even though no-one has wondered why
there were so few of us this spring

IN SLEEP NEXT TO BLACK BODIES, 2019

in sleep next to black bodies
gifts of love and worship appear to me
scribes, pharaohs, golden queens
silver, turquoise, lapis lazuli
the dwarf god Bes
Horus, Isis, Osiris
chariots adorned with flowers
lotuses saluting the sunrise
water lilies bowing at sunset
visions of black panther skin
moonlit Nubians
linen-clad lithe frames
luxuriating along the river banks
gazing at planets, the moon, amethyst stars
sending epigenetic messages throughout history
singing, praying, imprinting memories
ancestors walking past crocodiles
through papyrus
their candlelit wishes atop the Nile
floating into the future to me in dreams

NDN SUMMER, 2020

Blood. Water. Women. children
With flaming red kisses and yellow fry bread hugs
There is love you can taste wrapped in a paper towel waiting for me
In spring, I sit with white-haired women and grey rabbits
During summer, my cousins and I are every shade from walnut to brick
Our sweet potato skins roast on beaches
by the Feather and Russian rivers
Winters bring quiet nights with stories, singing, warm drinks, rice, and
red beans
Fall nights of steamy hot springs adventures alongside Yurok or
Chumash men with soft smiles and thick hands
Each season, my native body radiates alchemies of survival
Creates home-cooked potions to renew
Family-style resilience and communal roots
I am the safest amongst my histories
Creating chaos in the soil
Through reverence, sacrifice, altered states of consciousness,
drumming, dancing, and intimacy

TRAUMA IS A SOMATIC RUST STAIN, 2014

an opalescent intersex octopus makes its way out of the gender jar meant
to house it
they juggle eight anchors of socialization using slimy suctioned hands
and centuries of black fathers and indigenous grandmothers scuttle by
with plantations, rez trailers, and FEMA shacks atop their backs
 the life-preserving womanhood they float on
guides choppy seas of sexist storms
builds tsunami proof shelters
using transmisogynistic trash
opals of intersectional oppression
seafoam femme
sapphic sirenas
and the ancestral abalone secrets of swimming in both seas

PART 2:
LOST AND FOUND:
AIDS, LOVE, AND GRIEF

DEMENTIA PANTOUM
(ALL OF MY UNCLES ARE DEAD), 2013

all of my Uncles are dead
dozing with visions of William Shatner's corpse under their beds
dementia has twisted each of their lives into fever dreamt surrealities

made them forget friends, lovers, and five year old me
dozing with visions of William Shatner's corpse under their beds
tangled in dryer sheet thin blankets reacting to experimental AZT meds
made them forget friends, lovers, and five year old me

as I sat next to their hospice beds reading kids books about grief
tangled in dryer sheet thin blankets reacting to experimental AZT meds
dementia has twisted each of their lives into fever dreamt surrealities
as I sat next to their hospice beds reading kids books about grief

all of my Uncles are dead

DO YOU REMEMBER THE AIDS WAR?
2019

over and over, time and time again
quaaludes
sequins
boas
platforms
mustaches
wigs
dick printed Levi's
hankies
rush
cockrings
disco
Lou Sullivan
Alvin Ailey
Klaus Nomi
Keith Haring
Jerome Caja
over and over, time and time again
sweat-soaked washcloths
5A/5B
St. Vincent's
bedsores with cold hospital food
warm jello
used latex gloves
disappearing party guests
sunken cheeks
rice paper skin
red grape Kaposi sarcomas
the gasping and gaggin'
springing up mid-sleep to spew into trash-bins

hair finer than a dolls
no more gulping 1 AM milkshakes at Grubstake
farewell post-show cruising in the Lorraine Hansberry Theater
goodnight snap queens, banji boys, hair fairies, shady conspirators
trading laughter in cafes, bathhouses, gyms
for death rattles of fluid and phlegm
funeral bands played, and the choirs sang the mourners came
over and over, time and time again

PUPPY LOVE (INSPIRED BY JUSTIN CHIN'S "ZOO ANIMALS"), 2015

Welcome, Home.
under a full autumn moon, we are running in our dreams
and with tiny paws racing across the bed sheets
we sleep cradled in each others neck, scruff enmeshed in creature comfort
curled up on our wagging tails, at rest for once

Unhappy Accidents.
a junkyard tale of two young pups who sniffed, rolled, and bit
                                           (sometimes too hard)
play/ed, lick/ed, bark/ed, snarl/ed
and tried tried tried to take one another into the other's pack viciously
in that way, wounded and scared dogs do:
  panting
      drooling
         tail chewing
            ferocious ways

Old Yeller Ending.
canine clumsiness embodied
each night trying to find our way home
only to stand growling, waiting, and whimpering
on opposite sides of a doggy door that cannot swing either way 'til your
house is puppy-proofed
or
I stop foaming at the mouth

FOR CALLOUTQUEEN AKA MARK AGUHAR, 2012

It is so very complicated because she left us in Spring
chose to sleep in forever
because no one was ever going to be worth her "strength, love, & rage."
brown bitter queen; canonizing critical flippancy
too valid and self-esteemed
for this astral plane
a virally shared litany to her heavenly brown body
pansy face, soft and persimmon-like
contoured cheeks painted for the fatherfucking gods
hair in an imperfect top knot
and femme venom lips forever lipsyncing for their life
on Tumblr
on Facebook
Twitter and Instagram
in classrooms
lecture halls
zine fests
art openings
the entirely deconstructed life installation

GOOD MORNING GORGEOUS, FOR SYLVESTER, 2020 (POST-RONA)

"It would be so nice to have somebody to wake up to in the morning. But where am I gonna find a boyfriend, hobblin' around and lookin' strange?" - Sylvester on dating with a chronic condition [AIDS]
"Where am I gonna find a lover?" chirps the black queer songbird
without a conductor, the gay white band simply played on after she flew
from the stage
An open birdcage still sitting empty over thirty years later
A prissy peacock with geometries of sound and screeching colors
Sylvester made us feel mighty real
"Who am I?! I am Sylvester!"
Seeing! Swishing! Singing in Gay praise!
Soaring and tumbling in waves
fighting off scavenger men twice her age
Flying high into San Francisco's Disco lights
With high-NRG mating calls and chocolate ganache skin that
influenced the whites
When we saw her light shining, it permitted us to shine too
Oh, twirl sister twirl like every headwrap, kaftan, jingle bracelet,
mustache, and tight [but not too tight to stick your hands down] pair of
Levi's
keep influencing the dancefloor. Never forget your light.
Rousing Patrick Cowley from his dying bed
Reminding people that black people get AIDS too
You are a star; a transformer shooting offs sparks
The masculine outer layer and a feminine inner layer
adjusting pitch and building to a crescendo
So, hobble baby hobble, there's room in this sick and disabled bird's nest
for you

PART 3:
TECHIE BECKY AND
START-UP STEVE

WORKPLACE BINGO, 2017

A puffy Columbia or Patagonia vest paired with sunglasses and shorts
electric skateboard
"I pay good money to live here."
"I hear this used to be the 'hood."
The illegal scooter rides on a pedestrian sidewalk
An empty refrigerator while making $4k a week
"I'm Jewish. I get it"
freedom of speech
"I'm not racist. I hate everyone."
"Could you get us some coffee?"
freedom of speech – free space
"you can't make me feel guilty for being born white."
hair touching
"affirmative action got you this job."
"did you grow up in the ghetto?"
"how do you shower with a hijab on?"
"will you speak on the women in tech panel?"
a felon security guard who demands credentials in an office area that
requires credentials to enter
"black people can be racist too!"
No, I don't wasn't to play cornhole
Oh, I don't carry change, but I've got the "I-handy coin flip" app
Another e-cal
private jets to Burning Man

WAYS TO STAY SANE DESPITE IT ALL, 2016 (ELECTION SEASON)

Communication

Awareness of Feelings

Intimacy

Trust Your Body

Negotiation and Collaboration

Healthy Boundaries

Compassion and Empathy.

Awareness of Time

Autonomy

Accountability

Patience and Forgiveness

Acceptance

FUN, Gratitude, and Optimism.

THE REPROGRAMMING OF A CITY, 2018

01101101 01101001 01101110 01100100. mind
backdoor Trojan horses within a city's grid
phishing communities and doxing residents
in a language not meant for local users
the motherboard knew nothing of the virus
economic malware coded by black hat hackers

01100010 01101111 01100100 01111001. body
outsourced corporate hires and ground floor employees stacked three
    and four high
in tiny dark rooms with nothing but the buzz of their external hard
    drives to warm them
co-living like brothers and sharing bunk beds like waifs
swapping microwavable meals using the same survival tactics poor folks
    are shamed for
existing on the normalcy of performative poverty
affluent avatars faking the funk while others relive childhood
    simulations in food desserts

01101000 01100101 01100001 01110010 01110100. heart
streets sparkling with upward mobility but littered with the broken
    bones of black and brown twitterbirds pushed from their nests
hoodies, a graphic t-shirt, jeans, and sneakers
once the gear of the criminalized poor
now downloaded by corporate clones to wear uniformly in both ethos
    and logic
while careening down the sidewalks made jagged by shifting tectonic and
    economic plates

01110011 01101111 01110101 01101100. soul
navel-gazing VR staring wire people with bellies full of Soylent and
    hubris
refusing to let their feet touch the ground
floating above us with limbs so eager to climb the ladder
that the city needs to be sped through
some were left behind when the shuttle bus took off. rolled over.
backspaced as daemons clickety-clack through the night and synthetic
    culture melts the 7x7 operating system.

AN ODE TO SFS CRACKED
A CONCRETE SMILE, 2016

Her grin is reminiscent of the wrinkles near my grandmother's mouth.
Now slack due to the hemorrhagic stroke she had
after Mercy Housing proclaimed
nearly $4000 a month was "affordable rent."
Histories Deleted. Applications Trashed—irretrievable Data
lost in the web of awareness.
Her body began to dissolve pixel by pixel brain cell by brain cell.
Shortly after her master files were corrupted, the commuter busses
gave me bronchitis.
In 2016, I couldn't breathe. Grandma woke up from her 30-day coma
but couldn't think, and my brothers got racially profiled on their way to
IT and WebDev jobs in the Financial District.

WHAT MAKES A GARDEN DIFFERENT FROM A GRAVEYARD? 2013

a wet sunspot that covers your skin and sends bullets of darkness
down the body
knots of magnetic energy and bubbling hot plasma
the mass uprooting farming out families
we plant seeds of compassion for our confusion
before it can flower weeds in the planter box
I am ready for open-air grow rooms between potted realities and raised
rhizomes
leaves growing sharper and stronger every day
using the flowers that have fallen from a collective soul
to assemble memories
of radiant petals and bulbs that sway in the wind
from the displaced, I grow
and while I didn't create these garden casualties, I will heal them
tend to the land I'm loyal to

FOR SAVVY TAGGERS WITH
AEROSOL BREATH, 2016

When I was young, I used to paint this town with Psycho City veterans
and New Mission legends
ink-stained fitted hat, skullcap, Ben Davis and Dickies slacks wearing
homies
We'd spend our nights walking & rolling for hours bombing anything
that stood still
Scaling overpasses, cranes, warehouses, rooftops, tunnels, bus yards

One-shot juvenile delinquent two hits of 415 love and three tokes
generation hyphy
Blastin' down Bernal, Clipper, Divisadero, Lombard, Haight, and
Valencia
Trust fund art bros, Mission-Excelsior Latinas, Queercore boys, refugees,
3rd generation Italian / Irish immigrants, skinny rich kids who looked
like rats and talked too fast but always had the best lawyers so we kept
them around

With cans clinking in our backpacks, we'd scribble prophecies on the
orange and brown MUNI chariots that stewarded us anywhere the
backdoor boogie or youth fast-pass could take you
Leather dykes, graffiti gurls, and party princesses joined forces with feral
punks and skate rats
rolling joints on the back of Marxist books and Zadie Smith novels
Spending slurry city summers sipping champagne with gentle giants,
dancing till we dropped with strippers and hard-bodied capoeiristas

We were comrades in ink connecting to our framework through
hometown pride, angst, and adrenaline.
Swapping kisses with Hennessy, Smirnoff, Corona, or whatever someone
could buy from the old Russian guy on Chattanooga St. who always

watched "That '70s Show"
Early mornings trying (sometimes failing) not to puke fighting over the last stale chip from Taqueria Cancun
Bonfires at Ocean Beach, parties at the conservatory of flower, the Potrero skatepark, raising hell in every one of the 220+ city's parks

Careening over, under, around, and through black books, buildings, construction sites, school desks,
With fingers on can-caps shrieking like banshees in the bay
Howling on the cables of the cities trolleys, atop overpasses jumping rope with mortality
Until we got buffed out
In old-school SF, tagging was a way to say, "Here I am."
the declarative click-click hiss to proclaim, "I am my city's scribe, the vessel of culture
and a fumigator of corporate untruths."

UNDERTOWS OF GRIEF
(POST-GHOST SHIP FREEWRITES) 2016

DEC 4TH

I can't stop thinking about the ship that my disabled body couldn't board on December 2nd
the little peg leg I've cursed since childhood was too feeble to climb the jigsaw stairs
So, I walked the plank home to my squawking parrot of a parent instead of disappearing
into a Neverland of stranger bottle swigs, couches, and houses
I know I am over tech, but I can't help but marvel at the fact that I protected myself to support a first generation American Boomer using an iPhone 4 she still has not mastered the volume settings on.

DEC 6TH

the clink of a keychain bottle opener that is no longer used because drinking just doesn't feel the same when you are trying to piece together what was there before, but so much is gone and is never going to be the same. passing a joint to the left, but suddenly there's no one to hand it to. helping my friend look for a new housemate while packing the room of her old one. I'm crying at: Aunt Charlies, The Stud, on BART + MUNI, Wendy's, during nap-time for the children at work, across from SGraffito, below the overpass, above the bay, behind parked cars in the marijuana dispensary parking lot, on the couch of my friend who is only alive because she got too high to make it out of her house after changing her lipstick six times, in the bittersweet arms of a former hookup who purposely missed the Uber I sent him that night to ghost me and avoid potentially becoming a ghost himself.

DEC 7TH

We don't know, no one knows what will come of this
But I see 36 artful origami—forever folded
protecting each other just as they did in life
using hugs, love music, and community; smiling up at the stars
embracing joy
I'll remember
Alex and Michela, two young cariños kissing
Chelsea in her outrageous neon outfits; girls swapping pink tipped
cigarettes
sweet gothbaby, Cash Askew and Feral's laugh bouncing off the walls
Alex with the cameras and young twin daughters; his fiancee Hanna
from Helsinki
handsome Johnny, the half pinoy DJ, who we all had a crush on
Draven, a 17-year-old arts-high school student who must've been pretty
cool
Ara in her tiny backpack. I want to memorialize them all as
constellations
 being caring with every beautiful thing in the galaxy
forever catching comets of sunrise in their drink cups
laughing together in nebulous rhythm forever
p.s. parties will *never* be the same but perhaps that's okay

A LUCID DREAM, 2014

three white tech busses hiss down Divisadero
two developers stand at my head
one local 38 plumber sends the drain snake down
and I choke
"stop! I'm still living here."
my declarations unheard
he plunges deeper
repiping my heart
left to beat in the streets
rather than housed safely inside me

ON THE WEIGHT OF BEING
A UNICORN, 2014

one of the best magic tricks developers have mastered
is social prestidigitation
I am magic too though
an archive of the people's memory
the living document of nerdy black, brown and yellow kids from the
Fillmore
human Siri of resilience
through mournful unions
my chest opens like the doors of a MUNI train, the old white & orange
one that looked like a 50/50 bar
I am a sidewalk smoke stain courtesy of SFPD on 6th St
a draconian lease dovetailing towards Midtown Park Apartments
and disappearing income documents I've already made appear twice are
sent through Mercy Housing's trap door.
Mimes applauding
I have the historical hiccups, and my ability to inhale is fleeting
but I remain charmed and enchanting, the unicorn

FOR KAMEYO IGE, 2017

when my grandmother's teeth crumble
around the white fish of the mainland
I want to replace them with the sugarcane of her youth
if only to make language sweet again
like persimmons that have fallen from the backyard tree
she has forgotten me, but I still sleep beside her house
waiting to be rolled over on every once in a while
if not in recognition at least in angry curses of a language
I can no longer speak to her with the acidic split of my new tongue

MORNINGS IN BED, 2014

heart blossoms blooming

like subcutaneous carnations

soft but pulled taught

beneath honey skin

above unbroken bones

each blow pollinating

as we twist on sun-soaked sheets

springing forward because we can't fall back

PART 4:
GENDER SECESSIONISM

INVISIBLE INK + DIVINATION, 2019

There are stories in black transmasculine bloodlines.
And within each gender obscuration.
Hides an invocation to share with the world
Assembled beside nostalgia, patience, and hormones
The humble soothsayers sit.
Willmer "Little Axe" Broadnax
Jim McHarris
Marcelle Cook-Daniels
Alexander John Goodrum
Each man bearing witness and communing with deities
Holding bows and arrows in one hand; glass syringes or mirrors in the other.
They inject spell-books in our bloodlines.
To remind us we are not the vessels we were born into

Seeing far into the future using the powers of prediction
They acted as oracles and constructed altars.
With two cauldron shaped scars to protect them
In gratitude, their disciples offer needles, binders, and mustache clippings.
Modest talismans, for the rites of the transition order.

VILLANELLE FOR THE VIOLENCE TRANS PEOPLE ARE SUPPOSED TO ACCEPT, 2018

trans people huddled around a trough
filling up on rancid media representation
presented as something other than slop

artfully asked to take what we can get
injection, integration, ablation, and castration
trans people huddled around a trough

misgendering morsels served on both ally and bigots stale baguette
eating piled plate upon plate of political purgations
presented as something other than slop

patiently waiting for butchers who expect us not to inspect
swill and corn fed assimilation
trans people huddled around a trough

are they ready to slaughter yet?
do they fear starvation?
presented as something other than slop

mass media manipulated mindsets
meaty medical and mental misrepresentations
trans people huddled around a trough
presented as something other than slop

A TOAST TO TRANS FAGS
OF ALL GENDERS, 2019

Here's to building communities around the Mission at bus stops, corner stores, and writing groups. Tiptoein' queer archives and pissy public restrooms in the Tenderloin, cruising South of Market in leather jackets, jockstraps, biker hats. A "bless your heart" for trans twinks and baby gays prancing around Castro popping PrEP like Pez and cruising for male validation in skin-tight jeans with pre-folded hankies in their back pockets. Ashe to the boys sleeping in Fillmo' on soft messy beds fitted with jizz stained sheets and weed stems. Precious are the not-so—very-tender queers, trade illusionists, banji boys, tiny tops wolves, pigs, and bears. The blouses, honey girls, bois, faeries, unrepentant butch queens, black studs, marimachas, dyke daddies, and cranky but not problematic tranpas, the FTMs, butches, thems, and non-woman femmes are holding space in cafes, pool halls, locker rooms, personal ads, or anywhere the flames of hookup culture burn. Lanky limp-wristed sluts and short, stocky dudes with tattoos on their skin grafts. Three oi's for hardcore boys with faded X-Ray Spex t-shirts and poppers burned noses, kudos to every bruised kneed person of trans experience with a bald head and hairy ass. Sacred are the trans fat and sissified — past, present, and future.

SINGING AGAIN, 2019

As hormones mix and multiply
My talent divides
-.-.-.-.- |===>
What impacts pitch?
Is it singing for myself by myself
relearning my instrument?
creating spaces between my ribs for grief, the loss of sound or motion
There is no power in a song without freedom and flexibility
My songs used to be tight and high
Now they are low and loose
Post-Rehab
Post-spiritual injury
Returning to health
With Therapy
Pathology
Avoiding imbalance + addiction
/yet still falling prey to it sometimes\
Like the drum, my timbre, range, resonance, and articulation dictate
perception
So how do I behave in the trenches?
And what does continual motion achieve beyond displays of hubris and
an able body?

THE IMPOSSIBLE BLACK TRANS FAG OR 32-SOME-ODD WAYS TO BECOME ONE: MASON J. TO ASSOTTO SAINT REACTING TO "WOMEN" BY NICANOR PARRA RESPONDING TO "MEN" BY ERICA FONG, 2019

The impossible black transfag

1. The Reaganomics crack baby
2. The one with no birth time, hospital, or daddy on their birth certificate
3. The one who runs their life on sick, sad, and crazy time
4. The one who changed their body to go to bathhouses but still dances like a girl
5. The one who vogues for mobility because Medicare took his Physical Therapy away
6. The bitch with infamy and no money
7. The one who doesn't call, write or text back till several business days later
8. The one who calls themself "ancestor in training"
9. The one who can be "top daddy" or "baby boi," "papi," or "mistress"
10. The long-haired sissy one running from the endless pursuit of mandingo and cholo fantasies
11. The one who will stop at nothing to read people backward like the Torah
12. The one with limited white agendas and infinite hood solutions
13. The one who regularly breakfasts on *In the Life*," two hits of Jungle Juice, & a handful of fun-sized candy merely because they can
14. The one who bats their eyes three-or-four nights a week at the bar but always goes home alone

15. The impossible black transfag
16. The one who is Kermit, Miss Piggy, and Gonzo in a threesome with Felix the Cat playing voyeur in the corner
17. The one who is crunchy on the outside and soft in the middle, like Chicken Kiev
18. The one who can't safely lift more than 15lbs in the gym
    ...but wouldn't care to do if they could
19. The one who when they were 10 and 12, and 14 and 18 and 21 played in secret boys with who wouldn't claim them in the light of day
20. The one who laid under schoolyard benches hid in bathroom stalls and sat in matinee Rob Schneider movies to get kissed somewhere no one could see
21. The impossible black transfag
22. The one with the milky or cafe au lait partners and Dr. Pepper, graham cracker, elote, and yam skinned hookups too traumatized or saddled with karmic debt to ever stay for breakfast
23. The one who screams at chocolate, beans, curry, and rice queens on the apps
24. The one who wishes he wasn't an AIDS War survivor at 2, 12, 22, or 32
25. The one who is mourning their black faggot fore-fathers who didn't have enough time
26. The impossible black transfag
27. The one who still has his T-Cells
28. The one whose birth mama died of AIDS
29. The one who writes about AIDS
30. The one who sure talks about AIDS a lot for someone who ain't got AIDS
31. The one who acts up online but can't ACT Up in the streets with the middle class
32. The one who acted out of pocket said and did too much right here in front of each of you on this page
33.

WALKING WITH WOMEN OF COLOR WHO STARE AT THEIR FEET WHEN THEY'RE ALONE, 2014

HEAD. For coupled decades in two different centuries, I stood with a slouch, my hunched frame so calcified no amount of therapy or assistive devices could uncoil the outside world's attempts at social wiring. It took twenty-five-years 'till biohacking helped me stand upright. The truth is my bad posturing wasn't easily corrected because it wasn't birthed from genetics, accident, degeneration; I was bent from the injury of impersonating a woman.

SHOULDERS. This is for the bent bodies of women of color from my *pelirroja mestiza prima* to my Pepsi skinned Senegalese *playsista* for the cunts that no cat-caller could colonize; sistas who sleep in silk headscarves, *mijitas* with glowing Jesus portraits swirling above their beds. This is an ode to your orbital hair, your full eyebrows, and sideburns, your stretch marks; a sisterly slouch—tough girls who smell of gummy cherries, Hennessy, pink lotion [baby and hair], Palo Santo, and Sage it is for you, my other selves my former selves I stand the tallest today; eyes alert, head high, birdlike chest out, and fist balled to slug any man who dares to get too near either of us.

KNEES. I tried to find the balance between the two spirits in me for years, but as tender souls tend to be, I was fool-hearted, and men's gaze was intense enough to fold me like a table napkin. From the time I was old enough to lose my baby teeth, men felt compelled to aggressively pursue me (though these days, the concrete they used to corner me on divides our masculinity) Women with compulsions to scratch, rip, choke, and bite what they didn't like now clutch their purses when I am within eyesight. The 'round the way downtown girls who jumped me in playgrounds and at bus stops suddenly want me to be their token queer friend because I am no longer one of them. I am a reverse eunuch,

43

the self-exiled, dearly departed female secessionist; a chaotic gender-neutral—everyone you want to go to brunch with and no one you want to see alone at night.

TOES. Today I am following whom I believe to be the first man ever to try to put his hands on me without my consent. The only weapon I am armed with is a camera, so I aim the barrel at him, pausing only to notice how he is slouching in a cruel twist of fate. I am the one with power and no longer hunched over, so this time, he is the one forced to smile, and I will not let him go.

96,000 TO 47,000 /
CLOGGED GILLS, 2015

schools of kids traded sand dollars and grew legs in the good ole days,
baby girls turned double dutch with seaweed ropes
young boys surf'n turf danced atop the spirits of beaches
earning respect on the block and money to buy shrimp chips
non-binary sea witches swam from the deserts of sacred masculinity
into the cleansing waters of divine femininity
transgender seahorses did it all in reverse
mouths parched from patriarchy
all of them, aimlessly wading in the sea of gender.

PART 5:
FLOWERS FOR SNAP QUEENS

FOR MARLON RIGGS, THE POMO AFROHOMOS, ED MOCK, SYLVESTER, AND MY UNCLES, 2019

Tonight I adorn myself with
Cum shots and Cuban baby cologne
Murray's and Jam!
Two silver rings and my roped platinum chain

With a crystalline stud glistening in my ear
I kneel in a time-tested spiritual mating ritual to enter the church of a nightclub
speak in Tongues Untied
vogue to the ground in fits
as a DJ and host preach from their pulpits
On the dance floor, I am in Sunday School
Serving precision, poise, and a bit of penance

When the time is right, the parishioners will file in
Vers BQs in Champion and Nike shorts
Fem Twinks in mesh—perhaps silk or lace—
Chill Masc Trade with physiques by SoulCycle and political views by Milton Bradley
Amongst my brothers and sisters, I spread the good word
Spill the fellowship tea
Throw shade in morse code fan clacks
Praise dance and sing from the holy books of divas
Phyllis Hyman, Cher, Donna Summer, Patti LaBelle, Irene Cara
and our queerly departed St. Luther Vandross.

SEEDS IN THE SCHOOLYARD, 2018

Radicle - noun
Botany - the first part of a plant embryo to emerge from a seedling during germination.
Anatomy - a rootlike subdivision of a nerve or vein.

Radical - adjective (of change or action)
1 - relating to or affecting a subject's fundamental nature; far-reaching and methodical.
2 - advocating rigorous political or social change, endorsing a progressive section of a political party or extremist ideology.

ATHLETES
all around the nation
tall sour grass students with stems half their body length
scatter dirt on white-owned fields
watch them play, vying for the shot
to be put in porcelain pots
shining inside big screens and ivory tower nurseries

ARTISTS
boyish birds-of-paradise with dreads strewn atop their heads
flop around like clowns in flowerbeds
providing laughs; entertainment in morning-glory
locked in greenhouses, come nightshade
goofy purple gummed and orange grins swapped out for clenched jaws
rotting walls, loose monochrome jumpsuits

AFTER-THOTS

full-bodied girls in pajama pants with missing edges and faces like viola
northern lights
are demonized for being too hard to maintain, "just too much work."
watch them wilting into heat-stroked tiger lilies
spotted, weathered, drooping pitifully
bearing the brunt of society's failure to seed

ACTIVISTS

in the schoolyard, there are sunflowers
flooded with the poisons of the earth
yet shooting toward the sky
sharp minds blooming
unable to be weeded out of the garden; destined to toil the soil we pay
our plot fees;
stay alive despite repugnant rodents trampling our leaves

THE BEST TIME TO SEED FRUIT IS LATE AUGUST TO LATE SEPTEMBER, 2016

Last Fall, I tended to the orchards in their body for ninety days
became a cyclone spreader of intimacy, I drop spread seeds of passion
together we grew, tugged at the roots of one another
leaning against young trees of connection, we lapped up juices
mango, honeydew, and fermented guava

the fire in our bellies would have scorched the whole crop
but the mists of romance kept us cool
their watermelon mouth and my clementine stem arms
dripping nectar from ashy plum elbow to grapefruit nail lunula

a type of liberation that only comes from two brown-sugar babies
meeting in the middle row to harvest
despite dysphoria, distress & diasporic disasters
& before the floods of bleach that eventually split us like pomegranates.

PART 6:
HAIKUS 2010 – 2020

one grain of brown rice
unusual but welcome
like a stranger's kiss

blue moon bruises
sprang up from rose city roots
beneath Lake Merritt

there is something sweet
about the crying, we do
when our shoulders touch

amidst loss and lust
we sank under Mission Creek
and shared rescue breaths

barflies never know
how much they need queer spaces
until they lose them

under the harsh weight
of their father's old peacoat
I broke like chopsticks

when you walked away
glaciers formed and sent me
waterlogged visions

fog-swaddled windows
helped my shyness buzz off
with throat chakra songs

there are galaxies
and gargoyles in my mouth:
which ones need more air?

PART 7:
THIS IS YOUR MIND ON CORONA: ALL POEMS WRITTEN IN SUMMER/FALL 2020 AMIDST RELEARNING TO READ + WRITE DURING COVID-19

NATIVE ECHOLOCATION IN THE TIME OF CORONA

I.

I'm always amazed at how indigenous people find each other
I reckon it is all we've ever known
the answer is in the water
down where the sky people sent us to incubate since after all
 earth is accelerated light-work

We are learning so quick and sloppy that other astral travelers lock their
spaceship doors when driving by us
they overt all of their eyes because we're the sundown town of the milky
way

II.

the stars tell me we are stuck at the galactic kid's table due to our badass
ways
however, some of us chose to come here
to do work on ocean floors where there is healing
oh, just imagine the love for humanity it takes to be incarnated black
to risk swimming to land to support everyone and their literal mamas

III.

sharing the waters of our finding
knowledge of dolphins singing praise songs
octopi teaching telekinesis
fighting lessons from rainbow mantis shrimps
With our hair ties made out of kelp
And flat-chested crab goons protecting the block
let these mermaids keep singing white sailors to their deaths

THE BEST PROTEST IS BEAUTY

It started with texting a crush while viewing dahlias
swaying gently in GGP.
Fans blowing on me and the roses at Divisadero Florist
The last batch of Happy Boy marigolds from 24th Street.
Then came the lilies, stolen with held breath and
one quick snip from Cole Valley

There was Lavender, and Jasmine picked on my 2 AM walk
to buy Limon Lays.
And from my ndn brother-friend a gift of California Sage.
Kelp, Zinc, Osha, Bee Pollen
Shooting Star Botanicals, Thank you, Flower Medicine.

I hang Chamomile Eucalyptus Rosemary
Sip Mullein, Mugwort, Mint in teas
Perhaps Calendula, Carrots, and Turmeric will do the trick.
Angel Quartz, Larimar, Lapis Lazuli, Bismuth
Fiery Wall of Protection, Florida Water, and Palo Santo sticks.
Seaweed, homemade lube, and CBD

Right now, I am practicing everything I know about SF
to support me as one of its last remaining heyoka vertebrae
I am strong; I am in place. This is not my first plague
I am housed, I am fed, I have reasons to pray
But how many things of God are in question each day?
There are fires, separated families, incarcerated men, missing and
murdered indigenous women, targeted trans people. Even fake liberal
California is not exempt from our massacre of two spirits and 150k dead
in the gold rush.

I WILL HEAL–PRAYERS TO THE WIND

Oh Mama Oya! Our Lady of La Candelaria.
I offer you eggplants, pennies, and red wine
To thank you for the lessons of this place and time
Brisk as it is, your wind brings new growth
Destruction of what our planet no longer wants
Daughter of Yemaya
bringing down the deadwood, making room for review,
Swinging a machete clearing paths to heal and undo
She who turns and changes
The inspiration that creates or takes life
Pulling down the fences of ICE detention centers
Blowing over tanks in war zones kicking up sand at protests
Ushering the dead to their resting places

E.R. FREEWRITES 1 & 2

My lungs inspire courageous acts, goodness, and humility
A will to change cast aside arrogance, gossip, and bullying
The way the expand and contract
reveals transformation order and progress
It is normal not to know and rational to be afraid
Exchanging energy to create because delight balances plagues
We must continue to be warriors and birth this new world through grief
Doing laps around the planet with my hyphy cousins' Rain and Fire
While jealous, Aunty 'Rona pushes the getaway hoopty
They all overstay their welcome in my organs through emotional distress
But after ghost ridin' with them, I realize my held breath is best

8hrs later I'm home home
After consulting my oracle cards and having my partner pull tarot I
choose a hospital by fire watching (literally saw the building I went to in
3pt perspective via a candle flame) I calmly arrive at sunset to an empty
ER right before a rush of very sick patients....I help the Habesha elder
choose a stylus after she asked what mine was because she'd never seen
one used, a very bored lesbian checks me in and we cackled about the
MLB using cutouts of dogs as spectators, I explain PreP to a fresh outta
school triage nurse, everyone is stressed but I ground the rooms so they
moved a little slower with me, I lead my nurse in 4x4 breathing and
recommended bag balm for their mask chaffing all in all my visit was
about 7 hours and not too scary. I even charmed my doc into getting me
a rapid covid-19 test although I hear they're inaccurate. I only write all
of this because this is the labor disabled black trans bodies have to take
on to stay alive in the ER. This is what a lifetime of fighting to be treated
manifests. Although most of my symptoms never made it into the notes
or my chart people seem to be trying their best. Didn't leave with any
answers just "see a neurologist, isolate more, check your liver, monitor
your heart, and get into the UCSF #ehlersdanlossyndrome clinic"

There are too many questions I'm on an acid trip quiz show "are you straight or gay?" "what do you need a commode for?" "why did you come in if your oxygen levels are 97%?" "where'd you get the [chest] scars?" "have you been tested for mold poisoning after 32 years of exposure to it?" then the doctor says it's time for antibiotics stuck into my fragile veins I wince knowing it won't hurt but my arms will be ruby tomorrow. Antibiotics down my gullet 3x a day *I'll probably get a yeast infection or UTI* they say I can't lose anymore weight and I know the rules so I comply and I'm discharged quietly into the fog and back into the city's arms, around the corner for a lettuce wrapped Mel's burger to fatten me up, & off to bed.

RELEARNING HOW TO READ/
WRITE AFTER CORONA #1

Where are we safe?
Amongst our history and memories
in an underfunded public hospital with no PPE
who is infected
Are you getting tested?
It is in your blood, sweat, tears
 even your jizz and nervous farts
Do you have the virus?
Who has the virus?
Who courts a virus?
Others are lying but I'm OK saying I had a virus.
I'm just wait(ing) for the day the gays all get corona ribbon tattoos
I am not ashamed of what science does or does not know about me
How did I catch it? the same way my ancestors got smallpox and the
plague!
by daring to exist in the same time and place as colonized clowns who
didn't want the "stress" or inconvenience of community and had to move
West to conquer something to feel important

CLASSROOM GUIDE

The below guide is a static tool that you can use in your classroom setting. There is also a dynamic version that will change over time and that can be accessed by clicking here: http://bit.ly/36KnT83

LESSON OVERVIEW

1.1—Lesson Summary

Part 1—Students will use text to acquaint themselves with Mason's language and identities

Part 2—The educator will guide an exploration, highlighting what students need to know to interpret the poems successfully. (a brief history of SF housing crisis, LGBT issues, and gender-based violence)

Part 3—Students will flip through three pieces chosen by the educator and offer poems they are inspired to create based on their own lived experiences.

1. DEFINE A PROBLEM OR AREA OF NEED

Related Activity:

Part 1: Read Aloud–Think Aloud

Part 2: SF as Grandmother

Relevant Documents:

Artist Bio + Poem

Outcome:

Class discussion

Students understand the city as a matriarch, classroom as a flowerbed and helicopter as a vulture.

2. DISCUSS YOUR FAMILIARITY WITH THE PROBLEM OR NEED

Related Activity:

Part 1: Read Aloud–Think Aloud

Part 2: Building

Relevant Documents:

Vocab: Glossary Poem

Three things they love three things they want to learn more about

Outcome:

Class discussion

Students begin to understand persona poetry.

3. WRITE A POEM

Related Activity:

Part 1: Small Groups

Relevant Documents:

Exploration of neighborhood or hometown

Outcome:

Exercising the power of story and sharing the history

4. CONNECT WITH OTHERS

Related Activity:

Part 3: Presenting poems

Relevant Documents:

Student creates poems

Outcome:

Students will gain or strengthen a sense of pride in their places of origin

ACTIVITY INSTRUCTIONS

This section will break down specific, executable instructions for a teacher to reference during class. A few steps will typically be the same for all lessons, such as in the reading activity:

4.1— Reading

1. Pass out the *poem* to each student. Pass out the bay slang worksheet to each student.

2. Explain to students that the words on this page are critical for the upcoming story. Ask students to rate their knowledge of each word by circling a number in the "Before" column for the term.

   a. Read each word aloud and have the class repeat the word aloud.

   b. Explain the following rating system to the students:

      1 — I have <u>never</u> heard of this word before now.

      2 — I recognize this word, but I don't know what it means.

      3 — I sort-of understand what this word means, but I would have difficulty explaining what it means.

      4 — I can explain what this word means and use it in a sentence.

   c. Give students a chance to rank the word before moving on to the next term and repeating the process

3. Read the poem with the class, following the prompts in it.

4. Break into small groups to compose a single poem

4.2— Exploration Activity

Note: As an optional alternative for teachers short on time, one can skip the exploration activity. Instead, you can hand out the poem and walk your students through it either as a concise Part 2 or as the preface to Part 3.

Lesson Breakdown

2– RELEVANT INFO

Part 1: Reading Activity

Suggested Timeline 1

> Day 2, the first half of class

Suggested Timeline 2

> Day 1, the first half of class

Part 2: Exploration Activity

Suggested Timeline 1

> Day 2, the second half of class

Suggested Timeline 2

> Day 1, the second half of class

Part 3:Writing

Suggested Timeline 1

> Write

Suggested Timeline 2

> Share out

2.3.2—Part 1 *(10 minutes)*

This activity will take an estimated total of 10 minutes, during which the teacher will do the following:

1. Distribute materials to all students

2. Cover Slang/Vocab

3. Read Aloud

2.3.3—Part 2 *(90 minutes)*

This activity will take an estimated total of 90 minutes; that total is over two days. During this time, the teacher will do the following:

Day 1 (45 minutes)

1. Demonstrate the first part of the activity

2. Distribute material

3. Give students time to guess what the author's identity is

4. Discuss themes

5. Have students work on the poem in groups

6. Clean up

Day 2 (15 + 30 minutes)

1. Recap the second part of the activity that the students will do

2. Discuss results and answer discussion questions

3. Share results of the exercise

4. Share poems.
   Note: Contact author for presentation rates @
   masonjairo415@gmail.com

ACKNOWLEDGEMENTS

I am so thankful to everyone who kept supporting me and my work as I grew and changed ... bodies, brains, genders, zip codes, health statuses. Many thanks to the suckafree city and those who still hold that vibe yee! Weoutchea! To my beloved closed places of food, drink, and fun worship: Candlestick Park, Clown Alley Burger, Brother in Law's BBQ, Hair Jordan, Rafiki House @ Divis, Kiki Gallery, CELLSpace, Justice League, Coronet Theater, Pendulum, The Lexington Club, Esta Noche, My Place, Gangway, Lucky Penny, Zim's, Ms. Brown's, Bladium, Arik's, Health Haven, I-Beam, Park and Japantown Bowling Alleys, my darling, Asa for caring for me so deeply while I struggled with health, stability, and writers wages, thanks to my brain: going from very literate to illiterate and back to literate in 90 days, Natasha for lending her all-seeing editors eye, and JK for reminding me there is space to be both rugged and surreal as well as tender and sincere in this literary jungle. To my wordsmith heroes who wrote blurbs, booked me, signed my books, for everyone who contributed to the fifty eleven or so gofundme's that have kept me off the street and out of the morgue, I am grateful to all those reading I love you. I will not let you down, lastly to the women—my teachers, storytellers, and sheroes P. Smith, Rulan Tangen, Kumu Hina, Storme DeLarverie, Lenn Keller, Cheryl Dunye, Pam Peniston, Dr. Jennifer Lisa Vest, Gladys Bentley, Dolores Huerta, Lenore Chinn, Ruth Asawa, Kitty Tsui, Jewelle Gomez, Mickalene Thomas, Hulleah Tsinhnahjinnie, and the grandmothers Kameyo, Marie, and Pauline.

In 2020 Memoriam:

41+ Trans Folks in the USA
Leah Jahleece Norwood
Kevin Green of Esquire Barbershop
Stacey Park Milbern
JayR Rosemon

Lenn Keller
Diane DiPrima
Ruth Weiss
Monica Roberts
Little Richard
Tom Taylor
Alex Trebek
Haight Ashbury T-Shirts
Lucky 13
The Stud
Stork Club
Slim's
Au Coquelet
Cliff House
Gaylord's Coffee
It's Tops

Work Previously seen in:

Still Here SF (Foglifter, 2019)
MalaForever Issue #3 (2019)
RADAR Productions Blog
Locusts Vol 1. (2018)
Kevin Killian and Dodie Bellamy's *Mirage Periodical* (2019)
San Francisco Public Library's Poem of the Day (Nov. 8, 2020)

MASON J.

is an artist, historian, and community organizer, inspired by life as a born raised, and displaced Black & Indigenous San Francisco Local, Sick/Disabled Queer Two-Spirit, #PublicHealthNerd, and Land Use advocate.

Their photos, poetry, and social commentary have been featured in the National Queer Arts Festival, SF's Dia de Los Muertos 2020, Locust vol. 1, *Mirage #5: Period(ical) #2*, HuffingtonPost, Buzzfeed.com, *LA Times, SF Chronicle, Wear Your Voice, Vice,* and *Archer* magazines, around the internet, and at countless open mics across the US.

After holding the inaugural James C. Hormel LGBTQ Center Fellowship from 2017–2019, they did historical preservation with institutions from SF to Melbourne to ensure Queer History is documented. They currently serve as Program Manager for RADAR Productions, where they co-conceived Show Us Your Spines, a QTPoC archives residency with Juli Delgado-Lopera and Imani Sims. They're thrilled to be releasing their first [non-Kinkos bound] chapbook with Nomadic Press.

OTHER WAYS TO SUPPORT NOMADIC PRESS' WRITERS

In 2020, two funds geared specifically toward supporting our writers were created: the **Nomadic Press Black Writers Fund** and the **Nomadic Press Emergency Fund.**

The former is a forever fund that puts money directly into the pockets of our Black writers. The latter provides up to $200 dignity-centered emergency grants to any of our writers in need.

Please consider supporting these funds. You can also more generally support Nomadic Press by donating to our general fund via nomadicpress. org/donate and by continuing to buy our books. As always, thank you for your support!

Scan here for more information and/or to donate.
You can also donate at nomadicpress.org/store.